A Cat's Day

Luke had a very busy day planned.
He ate his breakfast quickly.
He didn't want to be late.

His old cat, Lucy, was
napping in the sun, as usual.

2

"What a lazy cat!" Luke thought. But he loved her anyway.

After breakfast, Luke got
ready to go to school.

4

"Don't forget to run my errands after school!" his mother called out.

"I won't forget, Mom!" Luke promised. "See you later!"

At school, Luke's teacher taught his class all about lions and tigers.

Luke could hardly believe that his Lucy was related to such fierce animals!

She was just too lazy!

7

After school, Luke stopped by the supermarket to pick up some things for his mom.

The supermarket worker was very cross. Someone had made a mess in the pet food aisle. "I wonder who did it?" Luke thought.

Next Luke stopped by the pet store to buy a new collar for Lucy.

"Maybe Lucy would like this ball," he thought.

"Nah, she's much too lazy for a toy like this!" he decided.

Around the corner from his home Luke saw his friend Sally in the clothing store.

"This store looks a bit messy today," Luke said to Sally. Sally agreed.

12

"Well, I've got to head home. Have fun shopping!" said Luke.

When Luke got home, he put down his bags.

He had a lot of homework to do tonight. He was going to write about tigers.

Luke noticed Lucy napping in her usual spot. She gave a quiet yawn. "How can that cat be tired?" he wondered. "She hasn't moved all day!"

Lucy looked up at Luke and yawned. She was tired from her day. "He'll never know about my adventures," she thought happily.

"What a beautiful morning," Lucy the cat thought.

"I think I'll have an adventure today!"

As soon as Lucy was sure Boy had left for school, she leapt out of the window.

"Silly Boy," Lucy thought. "He never notices when I leave!"

5

Lucy's first stop was her favorite tree.
It was always full of squirrels to chase.

"These squirrels can really move!"
Lucy thought to herself as she leapt after a
squirrel with a bushy tail.

Soon Lucy decided it was time for a snack. "I'm getting hungry!" she thought.

Luckily, she wasn't far from the supermarket. Lucy crept inside and tore open a bag of cat food.

8

"Yum! This is delicious!" she purred.

Then Lucy spotted an angry-looking supermarket worker. "Uh oh," Lucy thought. "Better get out of here! 9

Lucy visited the pet shop next. It was always full of toys, treats, and fish!

Lucy chased a toy mouse.
"Don't mind me, little
mouse," she meowed.

Next, Lucy slipped into the clothing store. She leapt into a basket of soft socks.

"This sock will be a great new toy!" she thought.

Then Lucy heard a familiar voice. It was Boy!

"I should get home!" Lucy thought.

Lucy got home just in time!
Boy was just walking in the door.

"He'll never know about my busy day," Lucy thought.

She settled back down in her favorite sunny spot.